Finding the Best Conductor

Testing and Checking

Leonard Clasky

COMPUTER KIDS
Powered by Computational Thinking

PowerKiDS
press

Published in 2018 by The Rosen Publishing Group, Inc.
29 East 21st Street, New York, NY 10010

Copyright © 2018 by The Rosen Publishing Group, Inc.

All rights reserved. No part of this book may be reproduced in any form without permission in writing from the publisher, except by a reviewer.

Book Design: Jennifer Ryder-Talbot
Editor: Caitie McAneney

Photo Credits: Cover Alexander Veprikov/Shutterstock.com; p. 5 yvonnestewarthenderson/Shutterstock.com; p. 6 Phol Thailand/Shutterstock.com; p. 8-9, 10-11 haryigit/Shutterstock.com; p. 12 Leigh Prather/Shutterstock.com; p. 14 ultimahule/Shutterstock.com; p. 17 Bomshtein/Shutterstock.com; p. 18 Sinisa Botas/Shutterstock.com; p. 21 Scott Rothstein/Shutterstock.com.

Library of Congress Cataloging-in-Publication Data

Names: Clasky, Leonard.
Title: Finding the best conductor: testing and checking / Leonard Clasky.
Description: New York : Rosen Classroom, 2018. | Series: Computer Kids: Powered by Computational Thinking | Includes glossary and index.
Identifiers: LCCN ISBN 9781538353189 (pbk.) | ISBN 9781538323960 (library bound) | ISBN 9781538355312 (6pack) | ISBN 9781538352878 (ebook)
Subjects: LCSH: Electric circuits--Juvenile literature. | Electricity--Juvenile literature. | Electric circuits--Experiments--Juvenile literature. | Electricity--Experiments--Juvenile literature.
Classification: LCC TK148.C53 2018 | DDC 621.319'2--dc23

Manufactured in the United States of America

CPSIA Compliance Information: Batch #WS18RC: For Further Information contact Rosen Publishing, New York, New York at 1-800-237-9932

Table of Contents

Making a Circuit	4
What's Electricity?	7
Studying Circuits	8
Closed and Open	10
Conductors	12
Testing Materials	15
First Attempts	16
Try It Again!	19
A Great Conductor	20
Check Your Work	22
Glossary	23
Index	24

Making a Circuit

Think about the last time you turned on a light. It was probably as easy as flipping a light switch. Today, the ability to use electricity is always at our fingertips.

Electric circuits are electricity pathways. They link a power source, such as a battery, to a device, such as a light bulb. If you make a circuit, you need to create the right setup for **electrons** to flow from the power source to the device and back again. Creating a circuit can take some testing and practice.

You can buy a circuit kit that has all the parts you need to create a circuit.

5

Electric lines bring electricity from a power source to homes and other buildings.

What's Electricity?

It's smart to learn more about electricity before you make a circuit. What is it? What can we use it for?

Electricity is a kind of energy that's able to flow through wires. It can power devices, like your TV, laptop, lights, and more. Electricity is made from turning other energy sources, such as sunlight, wind, or burning **fossil fuels**, into a new form of energy. After it's made, it flows through wires to your house or apartment. The electricity is measured in voltage. It can travel at the speed of light.

Studying Circuits

What are the different parts of a circuit? Many simple circuits only have four parts. First, they have a power source. Batteries are common power sources for simple circuits, but others might use a **generator**.

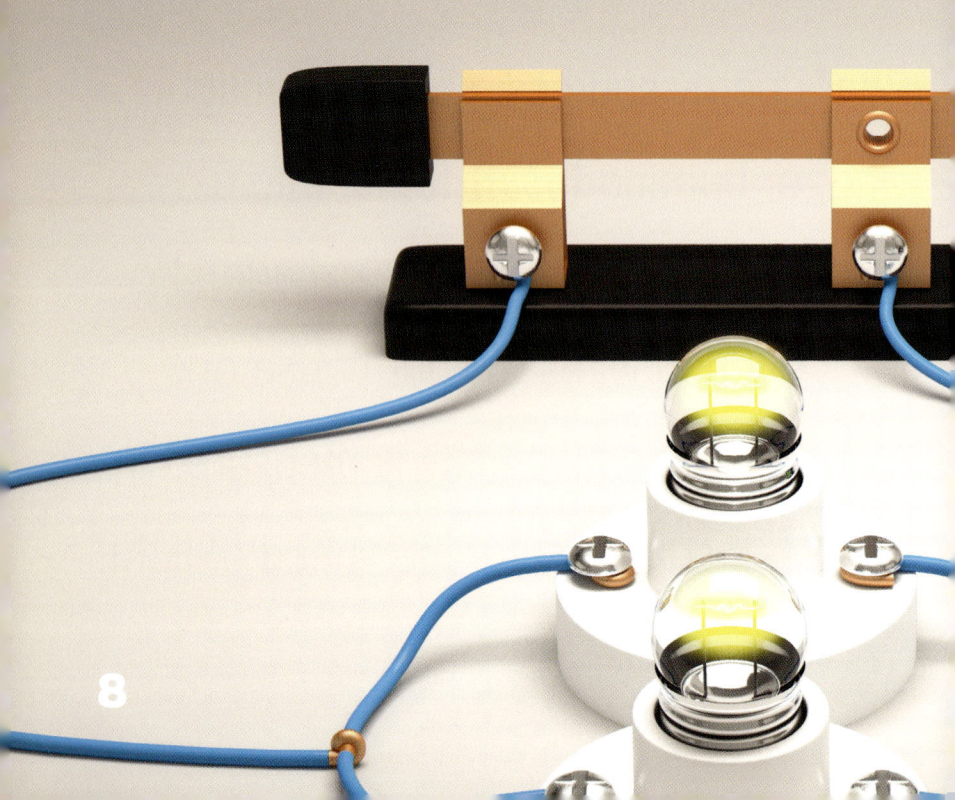

Circuits also have a device, such as a light bulb. This device will be powered on as soon as the electricity hits it. Simple circuits often have a switch that connects the circuit and turns the device on and off. Lastly, circuits need wires for the electricity to flow from one part to the next.

The wires in this circuit work as a pathway for the flow of electricity.

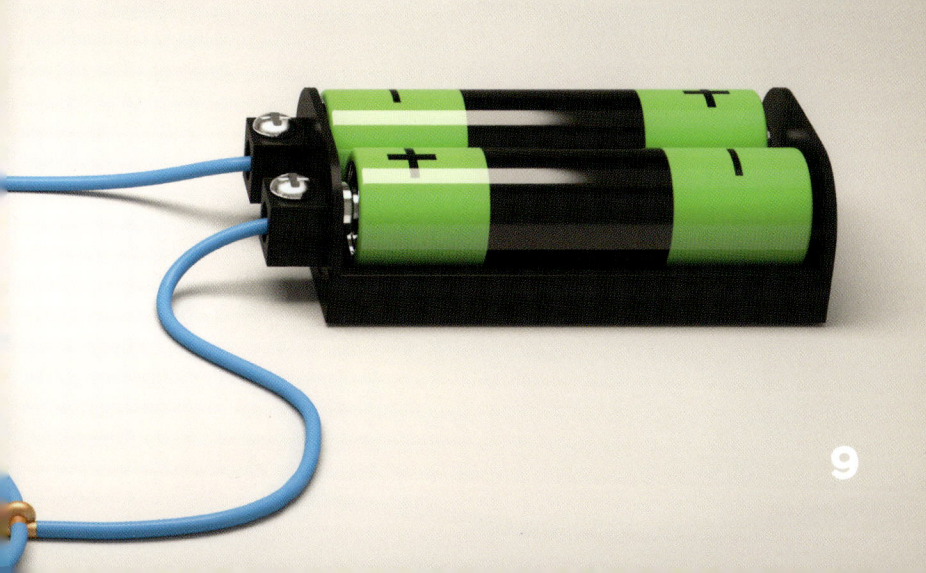

Closed and Open

The switch is the part of the circuit that controls if the device is powered or not. If the switch is closed, that means that the electricity can make a complete loop. The device will be powered on.

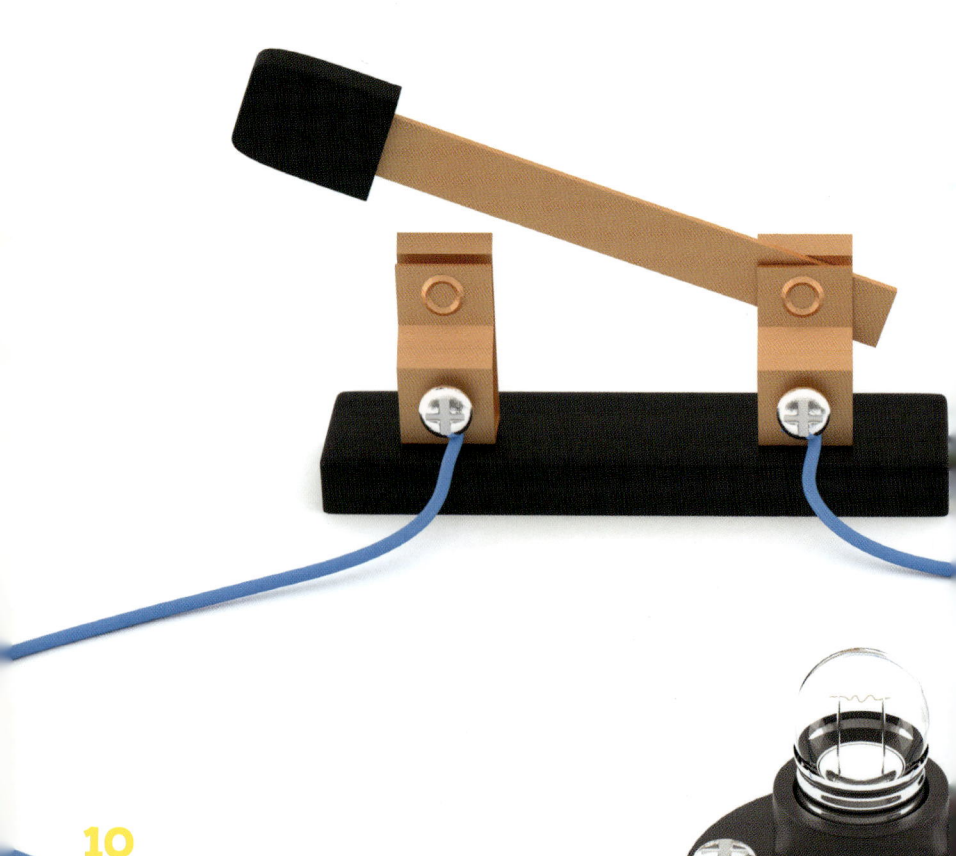

If the switch is open, then the electric current from the power source can't make it to the device. If the current can't make it, then the device will be powered off. The light bulb will not shine. If you ever have a device that's not working, check to make sure the switch is on first.

You can open the switch in this kit by lifting it. It's like turning a light switch on and off.

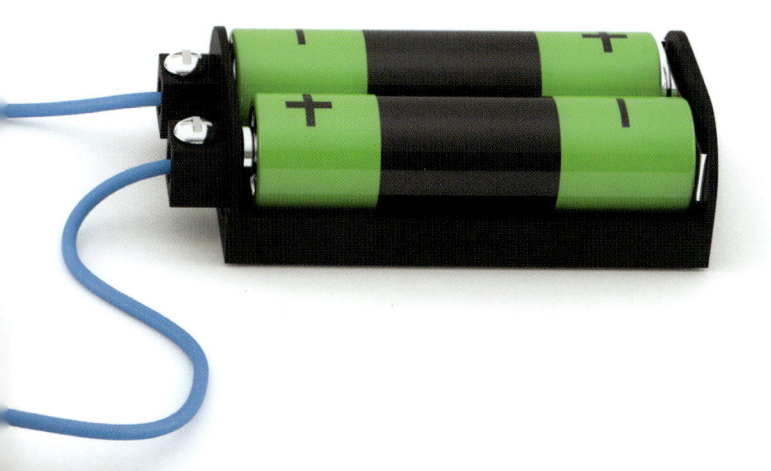

Conductors

Electricity can only flow through certain **materials**. That's because some materials are **insulators** and some are **conductors**. What's the difference?

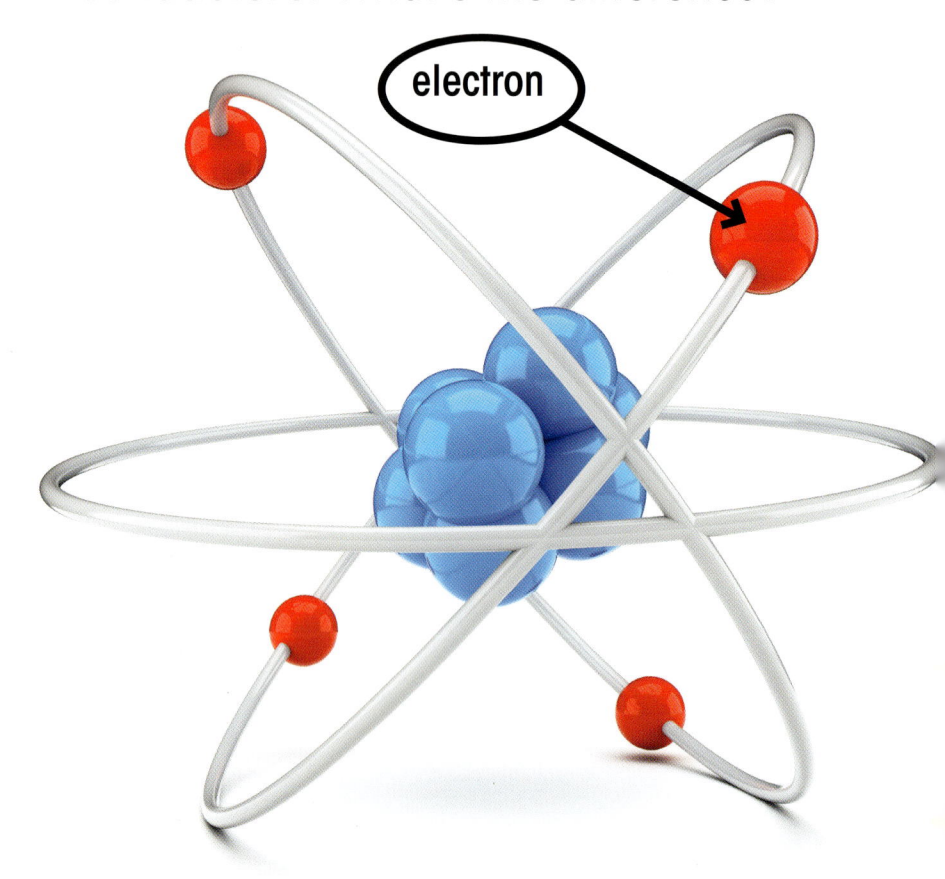

electron

It all has to do with electrons. Electrons are **particles** in an **atom** that, when moved to another atom, create an electric current. The atoms that make up insulators hold tightly to their outer electrons. That keeps electrons from flowing through them. Conductors don't hold tightly to their outer electrons, so they allow electrons to flow through them. Can you add an object to a circuit that will still allow the electricity to flow?

Electrons are the particles that are **orbiting** around the middle of the atom.

The kind of clips that are used with most circuit kits are called alligator clips. Their "teeth" look like an alligator's.

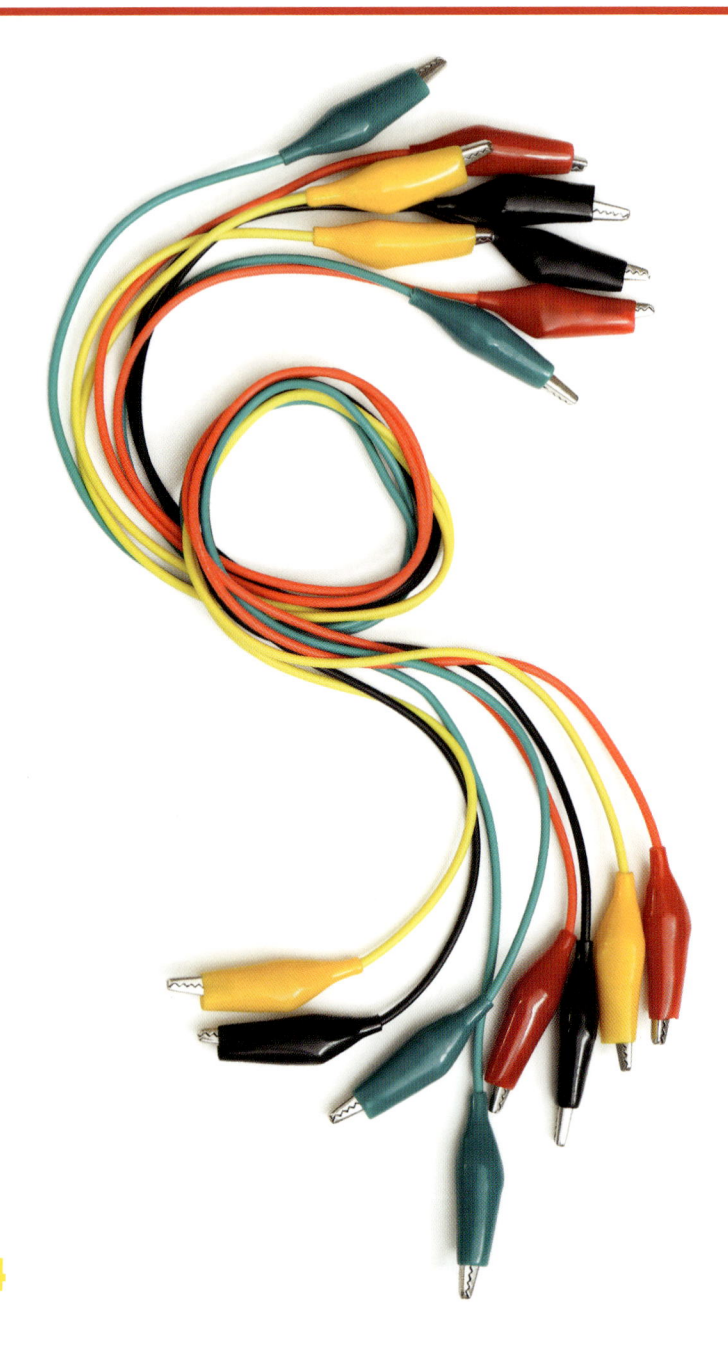

Testing Materials

Imagine you have a circuit kit. It comes with a light bulb, a battery, and **insulated** copper wires with clips on them. The clips will connect the battery to the light bulb, the light bulb to an object, and the object to the battery. In order for the circuit to be "closed" and work, the object needs to be a conductor.

You can test out different materials to see which will work as conductors. Materials might include a pencil, paper, an eraser, and a paper clip.

First Attempts

Imagine you connect a pencil first. Use the clips to connect the pencil to your circuit. You will notice that the light bulb will not light up. The circuit must be open because the pencil is stopping the flow of electricity. That means the wood of the pencil must be an insulator.

Next, you can connect your second material, a piece of paper. Imagine you put an index card between the clips. You will notice that the light bulb will still not light up. Paper must be an insulator, too.

Pencils and paper are both products of trees. They don't conduct electricity.

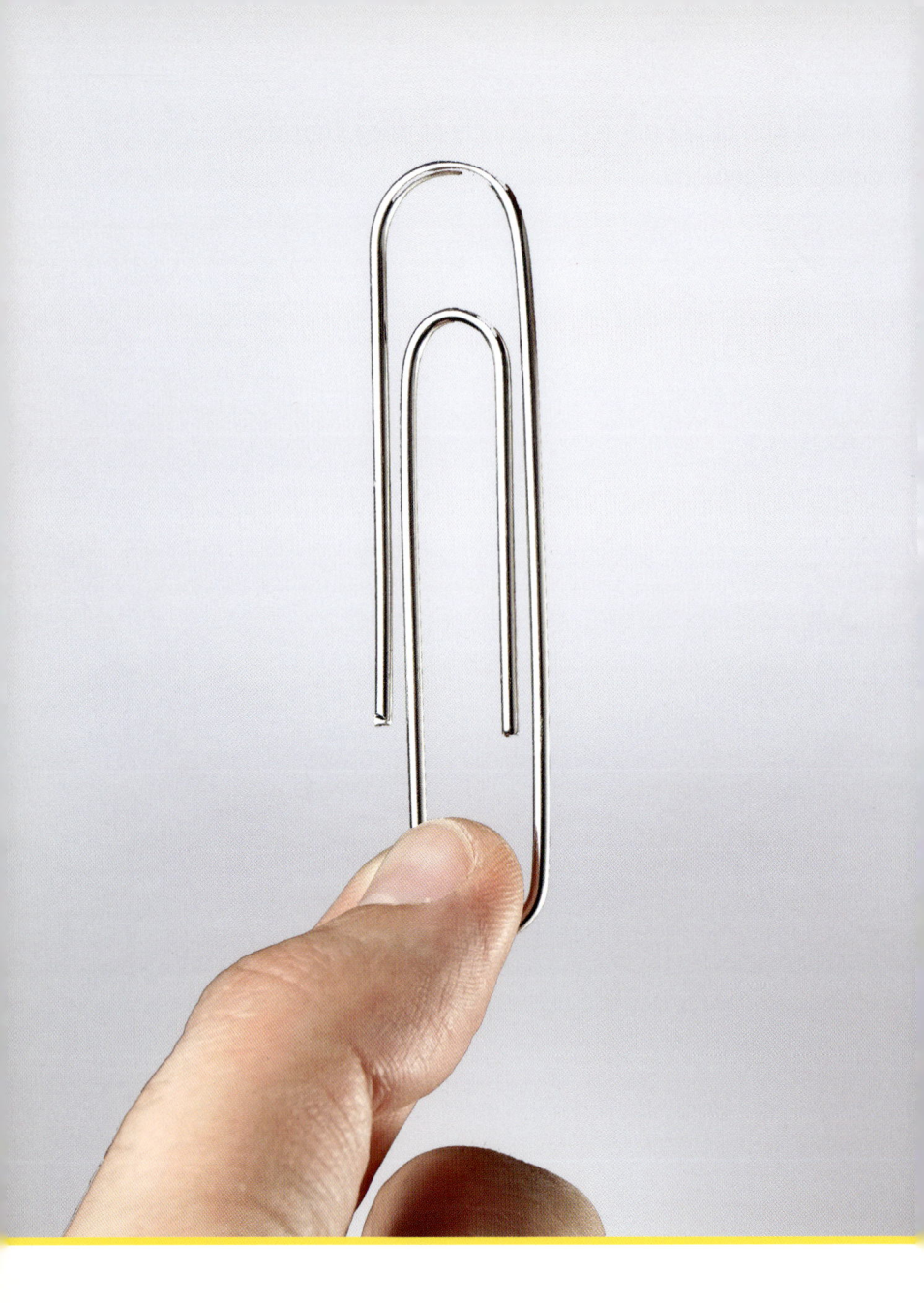

Paper clips are made of metal.

Try It Again!

Sometimes devices or experiments don't work the way we want them to the first time. If your first attempts don't work, that just means you have to try a new material.

Imagine you try to connect a rubber eraser to your circuit next. Is rubber a conductor or an insulator? You will notice that the light bulb still won't light up. Rubber must be an insulator. The last object to test is the paper clip. Connect the paper clip to the circuit. You'll notice that the light bulb lights up!

A Great Conductor

The paper clip will allow electricity to flow through it. This closes the circuit and makes the light bulb light up. That means the paper clip must be a conductor.

Paper clips are metal objects. Test out different metal objects to see if they are also conductors. Metal objects include coins, screws, and keys. Aluminum foil is also a metal product. Testing these objects will show you that metals are conductors. That's a reason why copper wire is used in making a circuit. Copper is a metal.

Different metals conduct different amounts of electricity, but most work well.

Check Your Work

Testing different materials can teach you a lot about what works in a circuit. Objects that close the circuit and allow electricity to flow are conductors. Objects that open the circuit by stopping the flow of electricity are insulators. You won't know if an object will work unless you test it!

Checking your work at the end of an experiment is important. Try conductors multiple times to make sure they work in your circuit. Then, you can record your results and educate other people on the science behind circuits!

Glossary

atom: One of the smallest bits of matter.

conductor: Matter through which electricity flows easily.

electron: A particle found in atoms that acts as a carrier of electricity in solids.

fossil fuel: Matter formed over millions of years from plant and animal remains that is burned for power.

generator: A machine that uses moving parts to produce electrical energy.

insulated: Separated from conducting bodies by means of nonconductors to prevent the transfer of electricity, heat, or sound.

insulator: Something that is a poor conductor, or matter through which electricity does not easily flow.

material: Something from which something else can be made.

orbit: To travel in a circle or oval around something, or the path used to make that trip.

particle: A very small piece of something.

Index

A
atom, 13

B
battery, 4, 8, 15

C
circuit, 4, 5, 7, 8, 9, 10, 13, 14, 15, 16, 19, 20, 22
conductor, 12, 13, 15, 19, 20, 22

E
electron, 4, 13

F
fossil fuel, 7

G
generator, 8

I
insulated, 15
insulator, 12, 13, 16, 19, 22

L
light bulb, 4, 9, 11, 15, 16, 19, 20

M
material, 12, 15, 16, 19, 22
metal, 18, 20, 21

O
orbit, 13

P
particle, 13

R
rubber, 19

S
switch, 4, 9, 10, 11

V
voltage, 7

W
wire, 7, 9, 15, 20
wood, 16